THE

BLESSING
OF

NUMBERS 6:22 – 27

By Barbara A. Perry

GARDEN 33 PUBLISHER
P. O. BOX 197
Aiken, S.C. 29802

The Blessing of Numbers 6: 22 - 27
by Barbara A. Perry

ISBN: 978-0-9960442-2-6

Unless otherwise noted, Scriptures quotations are from the King James Version of the Bible. Copyright © 1989 Thomas Nelson, Inc., publishers.

Printed in the U.S.A.

Thanks be to God for

My beloved spouse, children, grandchildren, and

family of Spirit of Prevailing Faith that keep me

in their prayers!

CONTENTS

DIALOGUE
(God's Plan)

The Lord: "If man will return unto me, I will return unto him."

Pastor Perry: "How does man return?"

The Lord: "With the heart -- A repentant heart."

Man Returns To God: *"Then shall ye call upon me, and ye shall go and pray unto me, and I will listen unto you. And ye shall seek me, and find me, when ye shall search for me with all your heart." **Jeremiah 29:12,13(KJV)***

God Returns Unto Man: *"And I will be found of you, saith the LORD: and I will bring you back from captivity, and I will gather you from all the nations, and from all the places whither I have driven you, saith the LORD; and I will bring you again in the place whence I caused you to be carried away captive." **Jeremiah 29:14** --- "For I know the thoughts that I think toward you, saith the Lord, thoughts of peace, and not of calamity, to give you a future and a hope." **Jeremiah 29:11** --- (KJV) "I desire to re-establish you in a wealthy place, to make you the head and not the tail, to bring you above and not beneath and to bring you over and out," says the Lord.*

Pastor Perry: "With what kind of heart shall man return?"

The Lord: "Man shall return with a clean heart. A pure heart – washed in the blood of the Lamb. A soul with a pure heart that has not given himself to idols nor has practice deceit."

Man Returns To God: *"Who shall ascend into the hill of the LORD? Or who shall stand in his holy place? He that hath clean hands, and a pure heart; who hath not lifted up his soul to an idol, nor sworn deceitfully."* **Psalm 24:3, 4** (KJV)

God Returns Unto Man: *"He shall receive **the blessing** from the LORD, and righteousness from the God of his salvation."* **Psalm 24:5**

Pastor Perry: "In what way shall man return?"

The Lord: "In giving."

Man Returns Unto God: *"Will a man rob God? Yet ye have robbed me, But ye say, Wherein have we robbed thee? In tithes and offerings. Ye are cursed with a curse: for ye have robbed me, even this whole nation. Bring ye all the tithes into the storehouse, that there may be meat (food) in mine house, and prove (test) me now herewith, said the LORD of hosts, if I [GOD RETURNS UNTO MAN] will not open you the windows of heaven, and pour you out **a (the) blessing,** that there shall not be room enough to receive it. And I will rebuke the devourer for your sakes, and he shall not destroy the fruits of your ground; neither shall your vine cast (fail to bear fruit for you in the field) her fruit before the time in the field, saith*

7

the LORD of hosts.   And all nations shall call you blessed: for ye shall be a delightsome land, saith the LORD of hosts. "
Malachi 3: 8-12 (KJV)

The Lord: "Giving releases *The Blessing* upon man."

Pastor Perry: "What blessing?"

The Lord: "The divine blessing from which consist all the other blessings. The divine blessing that covers the whole health and life of mankind."

Pastor Perry: "What does man receives from *The Blessing?*"

The Lord:
Sanctification (To be made holy and honored as God's children) – *The LORD bless thee.*

Preservation and protection – *The LORD keep thee.*

The presence of the Lord and joy in life -- *The LORD face shines upon you.*

Mercy and compassion – *The LORD be gracious.*

Kindness from heaven -- *Look upon you with favor.*

Wholeness -- in every area of your life -- this also includes: rest, harmony, serenity & calmness – *Give you peace.*

1

THE BLESSING

"And the LORD spake unto Moses, saying, 'Speak unto Aaron and unto his sons, saying, On this wise ye shall bless the children of Israel, saying unto them, The LORD bless thee, and keep thee: The LORD make his face shine upon thee, and be gracious unto thee: the LORD look upon you with favor and give thee peace. And they shall put my name upon the children of Israel; and I will bless them." **Numbers 6:22-27** (KJV)

The Lord Bless Thee...

God brings to Israel's attention or awareness that He is the one that cares for them. The Lord chose Israel as His people and set them apart from all the other nations on earth.   As His chosen people, He would be Lord God over them.   And if they were to be His chosen people He would sanctify them that they may be holy as He is holy. The other nations were considered unclean; Israel was not to mingle with the other nations, for God had set Israel apart as holy. God would cause nations to honor Israel as Israel honors Him. Israel was to look to God as their total supply; looking to Him to provide them with all the necessities of life. They were not to look to false gods/idols to meet their need.   God had taken them and join them to Him as His children. Their relationship was with Him, and they had to trust Him with their life if they were to continue in the relationship. The other nations of the earth looked to their "high gods" to provide their needs, but Israel was to look to and rely on the "Most High God".

The LORD keeps thee…

God made Israel to become His possession. He sat Himself as Lord God over them. His blessing was to keep them as His and not separation Himself from them. As long as they remained faithful to Him, He would keep them as His. He would protect and preserve them. He would be an enemy to their enemy and a friend to their friend. If they went whoring after other gods, He would separate Himself from them and not preserve them as a nation, but scatter them among other nations.

The LORD face shines upon you…

As Lord over Israel, God would not hide himself from them; He would cause them to see Him, as we see the sun. He would be their light guiding them by day, and their moon guiding them by night. His presence would be felt among them as the sunrays are felt. He would cause rain to fall upon their crops and refresh their dwelling places. They would have the benefit of delighting themselves in His presence. Their sons and daughter would enjoy themselves in the gates of the city without fear. They would know joy and laughter in its true form – within their nation. Contentment would be their constant companion.

The LORD be gracious...

God is a God of love, mercy, and compassion and He revealed these attributes to Israel. He would forgive them of their sins and heal them of all their diseases and He would punish them less than their iniquity deserved. Numbers of times God would have eradicated the Israelites, but through intercessory prayer he showed mercy and relented. God was gracious to us when He sent Jesus to die for our sins. *"But he was wounded for our transgressions; he was bruised for our iniquities: the chastisement of our peace was upon him; and with his stripes we are healed."* **Isaiah 53:5**

Look upon you with favor...

With God as Israel Lord, He would favor them above all other and cause other nations to do the same. They would be a prosper nation; so prosper that the other nations would envy them. Their gardens and vineyards would yield more increase than the other nations. They would be favored with wisdom to excel in life and in their skills, talents, gifts, and occupations above the other nations. Kings and Princes would show them favor in the courts.

Give you peace...

God is a God of peace, not tumult. When God took Israel to be His, He gave them peace (wholeness). Israel was to maintain this peace, so that they would not be broken in pieces and scattered over the earth. God wanted Israel to be a nation of peace looking out for the interest of each other. He wanted them seeking the good of each other. Seeking ways that they may aid each other in having peace of mind and peace with each other; such as, not adding interest to borrowed money, returning to their neighbor their lost goods, and leaving some of their produce in their gardens for the poor. They were to seek ways that they may bring rest to each other; rest from heavy loads and undo burdens. God desired that they keep harmony among themselves so that they would remain whole. He wanted them to be an aid in keeping and restoring each other to wholeness. They were to be in each other life as a river of serenity and calmness.

***

God's Blessing is designed for the whole person. God longs for us to prosper and be fruitful in every area of our life. God never intended for us to suffer lack on the earth. He wants His will done on earth as it is in Heaven. Heaven has super abundance and that is what God wants to bring us into – overflowing abundance. He desires that we be whole in our spirit, mind, emotions, body, finances, relationships, business and all else that life may consist of.

There is one big issue that makes *The Blessing* as solid brass over our head and as steel iron in our life and that is – SIN!

2

SIN BLOCKS THE BLESSING

"Behold, the LORD's hand is not shortened, that it cannot save: neither his ear heavy, that it cannot hear.   But your iniquities have separated between you and your God and your sins have his face (favor) from you, that He will not hear." **Isaiah 59:1, 2** (KJV)

When God hides His face (favor) from us, the roses don't smell as sweet and the sun sets in our life before it sets in the West.   When God's face is hidden – prosperity is hidden, jobs are hidden, businesses are hidden, and promotions and raises are hidden. The good things of the earth are hidden. The search for the good things of God – when His face is hidden from us – is like the person who search for gold at the end of a rainbow or like a prince seeking for an enchanted castle. Hear this, **"Though you cry out and though you search you will not find. The hill of prosperity is hidden and you cannot ascend," Says the Spirit.**

When we don't deal with known sin, it becomes our

downfall. Unknown sin also leads to downfalls and defeats. We cannot hide from the results of sin: known or unknown. Sin's results will catch up with us – sooner or later – and overthrow us in some area of our life.

Unrepentant sin makes the heavens as steel iron and the earth as solid brass. Sin in our life holds back heaven's blessings, but when sin is broken off we can receive a harvest of blessings and more answers to prayers.

Sin is a big issue with God and unrepentant sin will affect the flow of *The Blessing.* Our prayers to God will go unheard, the enemy will keep us bound, and non-favor will take the place of favor. Sin is an iron barrier between us and *The Blessing.* A multitude of curses will take the place of *The Blessing.* Misfortune will be as a companion to us. Poverty will be deposited into our accounts rather than divine prosperity. Sin diminishes our prosperity. Sin eats away our increase until there is no more. Sin renders us powerless to prosper and rise to the top. Sin keeps us beneath. Sin keeps God's hand from being active in our life. Sin removes God's defense in our life and leaves us open to be devoured by the weapons of the enemy, and the world. Sin causes us to be devoured by poverty, shortage, debt, and lack.

In **Joel 2:25** God acknowledged that He sent the army of devouring insects upon Israel. An army of eating insects that created a drought and famine:

"And I will restore to you the years that the locust hath eaten, the cankerworm, and the caterpillar, and the palmer worm, <u>my great army which I sent among you.</u>" (KJV)

In **Joel 2:12** God commands Israel to turn from sin that He may be gracious and merciful to them. (God will make our sins known to us, when we ask and in some instance when we don't ask.)

"Therefore also now, saith the LORD, turn ye even to me with all your heart, and with fasting, and with weeping, and with mourning: And rend (tear) your heart, and not your garments, and turn (return) unto the LORD your God: for he is gracious and merciful, slow to anger, and of great kindness (lovingkindness), and repenteth him of the evil (relents from doing harm)." (KJV)

In Joel 2:18 – 27 God reveals to Israel His loving-kindness that He will pour out upon them after they turn to Him with all their heart, and with fasting, and with weeping, and with mourning, and rending their heart (true repentance):

"Then will the LORD be jealous (zealous) for his land, and pity his people. Yea, the LORD will answer and say unto his people, Behold, I will send you corn, and wine, and oil, and ye shall be satisfied therewith: and I will no more make you a

reproach among the heathen: But I will remove far off from you the northern army, and will drive him into a land barren and desolate, with his face toward the east sea, and his hinder part toward the utmost sea, and his stink shall come up, and his ill savor shall come up, because he hath done great (monstrous) things. Fear not, O land; be glad and rejoice: for the LORD will do great things. Be not afraid, ye beasts of the field: for the pastures of the wilderness do spring, for the tree beareth her fruit, the fig tree and the vine do yield their strength. Be glad then, ye children of Zion, and rejoice in the LORD your God: for he hath given you the former rain moderately, and he will cause to come down for you the rain, the former rain, and the latter rain in the first month. And the floors shall be full of wheat, and the fats shall overflow with wine and oil. And I will restore to you the years that the locust hath eaten, the cankerworm, and the caterpillar, and the palmerworm, my great army which I sent among you. And ye shall eat in plenty, and be satisfied, and praise the name of the LORD your God that hath dealt wondrously with you: and my people shall never be ashamed (put to shame). And ye shall know that I am in the midst of Israel, and that I am the LORD your God, and none else: and my people shall never be ashamed."(KJV)

The message delivered to Israel is also to us. The army of devourer, that devoured Israel, is also the devourer that will be sent to devour us when we're in sin. The Blessing sent to Israel is also to Christians.

Christians have become partaker of the Old and New

Testament promises through Jesus Christ. It is written in **Ephesians 2:11-19**, *"Remember that once you were not Jewish physically. Those who called themselves "the circumcised" because of what they had done to their bodies called you "the uncircumcised". Also, at that time you were without Christ. You were excluded from citizenship in Israel, and the pledges (covenants) God made in his promise were foreign to you. You had no hope and were in the world without God. But now through Christ Jesus you, who were once far away, have been brought near by the blood of Christ. So he is our peace. In his body he has made Jewish and non-Jewish people one by breaking down the wall of hostility that kept them apart. He brought an end to the commandments and demands found in Moses' Teachings so that he could take Jewish and non-Jewish people and create one new humanity in himself. So he made peace. He also brought them back to God in one body by his cross. On which he killed the hostility. He came with the Good News of peace for you who were far away and for those who were near. So Jewish and non-Jewish people can go to the Father in one Spirit. That is why you are no longer foreigners and outsiders but citizens together with God's people and members of God's family." (God's Word Series)*

The *Blessing* is our birthright. When we were born again after receiving Christ into our hearts, we became entitled to all the rights and privileges of the *Blessing*. Although the *Blessing* is our birthright, we can forfeit it.

The *Blessing* is legally binding.

When we enter into a contract, we're obligated to keep it until it expires. We must adhere to all that is written therein, if not, we forfeit it or breach it – with penalties. If we forfeit it, we lose all rights to what was written in it. Sin is a forfeit and a breach. Sin causes us to lose all the rights to *The Blessing.*

> Forfeit is defined as something surrendered as punishment; penalty or fine. It also is defined as something placed in escrow and then redeemed after payment of a fine.
>
> Escrow is defined as a written agreement, such as a deed, put into the custody of a third party until certain conditions are fulfilled.

The something placed in escrow is the *Blessing.* The then redeemed after payment of a fine was Jesus death on the cross. The escrow was put into the custody of the third party (Holy Spirit: that administer the blessings) until certain conditions are fulfilled.

3

THE BLESSING IS CONDITIONAL

The Blessing is based on conditions being met. When certain conditions are met, the Holy Spirit rains down showers of blessings. The showers come down in seasons. The season may come that you really need showers of God's Grace, the season may come that you really need showers of His love, favor, strength or presence. Whatever season you may be in, if the conditions are met, you can expect the showers to fall. Your season may be a time of loneliness; you can expect God's showers of love, comfort, grace, or his presence. Whatever season of need you maybe in, God has what you need to make it through. Ask Him for it. Call upon His name and you will be blessed!

The condition for *The Blessing* is in righteousness, obedience, faithfulness, and the condition of the heart. God in His sovereignty releases the blessing in His grace and mercy.

Abraham's blessing was conditional: *God said unto him, "I am the Almighty God; walk before me, and be thou perfect (holy). And I will make my covenant between me and thee, and will multiply thee exceedingly."* **Genesis 17: 1, 2** (KJV)

Abraham had to live a life of holiness before God. A life that would bring honor unto God, a life of worship, and of integrity: a virtuous life.

The Israelites' blessing was conditional both in **Leviticus 26:1-13** and **Deuteronomy 28:1-14**. Covenant blessings, which Christians can now claim through Christ Jesus. Through Christ Jesus we are blood covenant people and have become the seeds of Abraham. And because we are the children of Abraham, we are heirs to the Old and New Covenant's blessings. It is written, *"You are all God's children by believing in Christ Jesus. Clearly, all of you who were baptized in Christ's name have clothed yourselves with Christ. There is neither Jew nor Greek, slaves nor free people, males nor females. You are all the same in Christ Jesus. If you belong to Christ, then you are Abraham's descendants and heirs, as God promised."* **Galatians 3: 26-29** (GWS)

The blessings in **Matthew 6:25-33** is conditional, *"Therefore I say unto you, Take no though for your life, what ye shall eat, or what ye shall drink; nor yet for your body, what ye shall put on. Is not the life more than meat(food), and the body than rainment(clothing)? Behold the fowls of the air: for they sow not, neither do they reap, nor gather into barns; yet your heavenly Father feedeth them. Are ye not much better than they? Which of you by taking thought (worrying) can add one cubit unto his stature(height)? And* *why take ye thought (worry) for raiment? Consider the lilies of the field, how they grow; they toil not, neither do they spin: And yet I say unto you, That even Solomon in all his glory was not arrayed(clothed) like one of these. Wherefore, if God so clothe the grass of the field, which to day is, and to morrow is cast into the oven, shall he not much more clothe you, O ye of little faith? Therefore take no thought (do not worry), saying, What shall we eat? or, Wherewithal shall we be clothed? (For after all these things do the Gentiles seek;) for your heavenly Father knoweth that ye have need of all these things."* **Condition:** *"But seek ye first the kingdom of God, and his righteousness; and all these things shall be added unto you."* (KJV)

The blessing in **Luke 6:38** is also conditional. It is based on **giving.** *"Give, and it shall be given unto you; good measure, pressed down, and shaken together, and running over, shall men give into your bosom. For with the same measure that ye mete (use) withal it shall be measured to you again."* (KJV)

Christians, *The Blessing* is here! If we want to turn the faucet of the Blessing on in our life, we got to do the conditions.

In **Isaiah 1:19, 20** it is written, *"If ye be willing and obedient, ye shall eat the good of the land: But if ye refuse (to be willing and obedient) and rebel, ye shall be devoured* with the sword: for the mouth of the LORD has spoken it." If you refuse the required conditions, God says you will be devoured with the sword. Swords of poverty that will eat up your life: destroy, consume, or waste you away. Struggle and lack will always be your companions. The swords won't be limited to just your finances but every area of your life. Your home, business, relationships, and health will all show signs of the sword of poverty. It is written in **Proverbs 15:6,** *"In the house of the righteous is much treasure: but in the revenues of the wicked is trouble."(KJV)*

When you live your life contrary to God's laws and principles, you are in the sin of disobedience, and God's curses will be measured to you. The curses of God for the disobedience in **Leviticus 26:14-39** is written below:

> *"If you will not listen to me and obey all these commands, if you reject my laws and look at my rules with disgust, if you reject my promise by disobeying my commands, then this is what I will do to you: I will terrorize you with disease and fever. You will suffer from eye problems and depression. You will plant your crops and get nothing because your enemies will eat them. I will condemn you so that you will go down in defeat in front of your enemies. Those who hate you will be your rulers. You will run away even*

when no one is chasing you. If you still will not listen to me, I will discipline you seven times for your sins. I will crush your arrogance. You will have no rain, and your land will be as hard as cement. You will work hard for nothing because your land will produce no crops and the trees will produce no fruit. If you resist and don't listen to me, I will increase the punishment for your sins seven times. I will send wild animals among you. They will rob you of your children, destroy your cattle, and make you so few that your roads will be deserted. If this discipline does not help and you still resist, then I, too, will resist you. I will punish you seven times for your sins. I will bring war on you to get revenge for my promise that you rejected. When you gather in your cities, I will send plagues on you and you will fall under the control of your enemy. I will destroy your food supply. Ten women will need only one oven to prepare your food. You will eat and go away hungry. If in spite of this you do not listen to me and still resist me, I will fiercely resist you. I will discipline you seven times for your sins. You will eat the bodies of your sons and daughters. I will destroy your worship sites, cut down your incense altars, and pile your dead bodies on top of your dead idols. I will look at you with disgust. I will make your cities deserted and ruin your sacred places. I will no longer accept the soothing aroma from your sacrifices. I will make your land so deserted that your enemies will be shocked as they settle in it. I will scatter you among the nations. War will follow you. Your country will be in ruins. Your cities will be deserted. Then the land will enjoy its time to honor the LORD, while it lies deserted and you are in your enemies' land. Then the land will joyfully celebrate its time to honor the LORD. All the days it lies deserted; it will celebrate the time to honor the LORD it never celebrated while you lived there. I will fill with despair those who are left in the land of their enemies. The sound of a wind-blown leaf will make them run. They will run away and fall, but no one will be chasing them. They will stumble over each other, but no one will be after them. They will not be able to stand up to their enemies. They will be destroyed among the nations. The land of their enemies will devour them. Those who are left will waste away in the lands of their enemies because of their sins and the sins of their ancestors."(GWS)

If you have been living your life in disobedience, unrighteousness, and unfaithfulness, then you probably can identify with some of these curses. If you desire to move from the curses to *The Blessing,* then it is only through Christ Jesus that you can be forgiven and restored. If you have not received Jesus Christ as your Savior but desire to do so, pray the salvation prayer at the end of this chapter. Through Christ you can become a child of God and partake of the inheritance of *The Blessing.* God will keep His covenant promise with you as He kept it with Abraham. When you come into the family of God, you move out of the house of curses and enter into the house of *The Blessing:* Jesus Christ is the entrance door. The Scripture declares,

"Christ paid the price to free us from the curse that God's laws bring by becoming cursed instead of us. Scripture says, "Everyone who is hung on a tree is cursed." Christ paid the price, so that the blessing promised to Abraham would come to all the people of the world through Jesus Christ and we would receive the promised Spirit through faith." **Galatians 3:13,14** (GWS)

SALVATION PRAYER

Lord Jesus, be merciful to me and save my soul. Lord, it is written in thy Word, "For all have sinned and come short of the glory of God." I am one who has fallen short. Sin has invaded my life; I need you to save and deliver my soul. I admit that I am a sinner. Lord, I was born into a world of sin. I need you to deliver me from this sinful lifestyle. I rely on your ability and not my own to save me. Today, Lord, I repent of my sins and ask you to come into my heart. Cleanse me and wash me white as snow as you said you would in your word, "Come now, and let us reason together, saith the LORD: though your sins be as scarlet, they shall be as white as snow: though they be red like crimson, they shall be as wool." Thank you for coming into my heart and life. I confess you to be the Son of the living God that died and rose again and sits at the right hand of the Father in heaven. Bless be you Jesus for being my Lord and Saviour this day and every day. Lord Jesus, I also need you to fill me with the Holy Spirit, that power I need to live this life and be a witness for you. So send the Holy Spirit to live in me now. Thank you Lord! Amen

Now that the issue of sin is settled, let's move on to God's ideal of increasing His people.

4

INCREASED GREATLY THROUGH MULTIPLICATION

In the beginning of creation, God's principle was to increase speedily through multiplication. When God created sea and flying animals, He released a command blessing of fruitfulness and multiplication: neither addition nor subtraction. *"And God blessed them, saying, Be fruitful, and multiply, and fill the waters in the seas,..."* **Genesis 1:22** (KJV)

God's spoken command to the living creatures was to be fruitful and multiply or increase greatly. I believe multiplication is God's ideal of addition. I believe He adds to animals and mankind through multiplication. When God created human beings, He released a command blessing of multiplication. *"So God created man in his own image, in the image of God created he him; male and female created he them. And God blessed them, and God said unto them, Be fruitful, and multiply, and replenish the earth...."* **Genesis 1:27, 28** (KJV)

God's first command was to be fruitful (produce fruits/results). To see that His command would be carried out, God deposited in animals and humans sexual desire and reproduction power. He joined male and female together in marriage that they may come together in sexual union. He also placed a timeframe or table of days or months that fruit would come forth as a result of their sexual union. At the appointed end of days or months the results would be delivered; some unions would bear more fruit, than others. And through their produced fruit, life would be multiplied with grandchildren and great grandchildren and great, great grandchildren. The generation of that produced fruit would continue to multiply: creating many descendents. God desires it to be on earth as it is in heaven – overflowing.

After mankind and animals had multiplied greatly on the earth, God sent a flood to destroy all living things, due to sin that had increased on the earth. After the flood had receded of the face of the earth, God's command to Noah and his family was to be fruitful and multiply. God's ideal of multiplication has not changed.

God's ideal of increasing greatly through multiplication flowed over to Abraham, Isaac, Jacob and their seeds. Read the history of the book of beginning as it is written in Genesis 1:22 & 28(animals and humans), 6:1(mankind), 8:17(living thing), 9:1&7(Noah and sons), 16:10(Hagar's seed), 17:2&20(Abraham and Ishmael), 22:17(Abraham), 26:4&24(Isaac) and 35:11 (Jacob). God's ideal of increasing greatly has not changed. If we are seeds of Abraham through Christ Jesus, then that blessing of multiplication is passed on to us. God believes in plenty. He's not a God of shortage. God has ten thousands of blessings to satisfy the poor. He owns the cattle upon a thousand hills. All the gold and silver is His and He doesn't mind sharing. *("Blessed be the Lord, who daily loadeth us with benefits, even the God of our salvation."* **Psalm 68:19)** (KJV)

Christians, I know that the Lord delights in returning unto us good things as we give our tithes and offerings to Him, but I was deeply concern because I didn't have a large amount of tithe and offering to give so I could receive out of the range of 30, 60 or 100 fold as it is stated in the Scripture. *"But other fell into good ground, and brought forth fruit, some an hundredfold, some sixtyfold, some thirtyfold."* **Matthew 13:8** *(KJV)*

Then the Lord said to me, "What we give will be doubled." As I was pondering on what He said, in earthly understanding I'm calculating 30/60, 60/120 and 100/200. If I gave $30 I'll receive $60 from God. If I gave $60 I'll receive $120 and if I gave $100 I'll receive $200. Now if He gave it to me that way that will be an addition. That will be good! I can increase from that. But if He multiplied it and gave it back to me I can increase faster and greatly. I could get more debt taken care of by multiplication then by addition. Then the Lord showed me what He was speaking of; which included, weighing the heart and its motives. The 40 I said, "The giving is multiplied according to my standard through the seeds of willingness, obedience, and faithfulness. *"Now he that ministereth seed to the sower both minister bread for your food, and multiply your seed sown...."* **2Corinthians 9:10** (KJV)

The Lord then showed me dimensions or levels of increase of multiplication. These levels are what He uses to increase the faithful sowers not the sparsely sowers. Keep in mind that it is God that gives seeds to sow, so that you can become a sower, just as he gave humans and animals the stuff needed to carry out his command to be fruitful and multiply. Remember, it all comes from God.

Our willingness, obedience, and faithfulness are seeds from God that determine our level of multiplication. These seeds were imparted into our spirit when we were born again. These seeds only benefit us in receiving from God when we release them. A seed is never profitable until it is planted in the ground. Once it is in the ground, it has the power to transform into something different and bear much fruits -- even multiplied fruit. *Faith* is the soil through which our seeds are exchanged into multiplied blessings.

When we make a choice and release the seeds of willingness, obedience and faithfulness, coupled with our tithes and/or offerings, we activate multiplication upon our giving. We release God's hand to take that seed and exchange it into multiplied blessings to meet the need.

As the Lord said -- He measures by His standard. I will now share a concept with you from the Lord. This concept is in no wise a formula for calculating a financial return from the Lord, but to let us know we can not out give God nor buy God, but God through His grace and mercy returns unto us.

THE CONCEPT

Let's say Christ started you on the 30-fold dimension level in giving tithes and offering when you first receive Him. You faithfully follow Him; you sow in faith the seeds of willingness, obedience, and faithfulness. So He multiplied you by 30, which could give you a healthy return of $900 (30x30=900). Sounds good but it gets better. Each seed comes with an amount. The seed of willingness equal 30. The seed of obedience and faithfulness equal 30. When each is double its return is 60 each. Your willing (60) times your faithful and obedience (60) equal $3600, but it doubles when you sow them in faith. That would then put you at $7,200 (3600x2). Christ then promotes you to the 60 fold dimension level. Willingness' seed equal 60. Faithful and obedience seed equal 60. When each is double, its return is $120 each. Willingness ($120) time faithfulness and obedience ($120) equal $14,400. Sow them in faith and that would put you at $28,800 (14,400x2). You continued on following faithfully and He promotes you to the over flow dimension level of 100 fold and higher. Willingness seed ($100). Faithful and obedience seed ($100). When double, its return is $200 each. Willingness ($200) time faithfulness and obedience

($200) equal $40,000. Sow them in faith and that would put you at $80,000 (40,000x2). After you reach the overflow level you entered into a greater dimension level. No longer are you being multiplied by 30, 60 or 100 but by hundreds and thousands. Your exchange is a dimension of divine prosperity and rivers of blessings.

The Lord said, "I gave you this concept because there are some chains in your spirit that needs to be broken regarding giving and receiving. Renew your mind to this standard of giving and receiving. Consider the widow's mite."

"And there came a certain poor widow, and she threw in two mites, which make a farthing. And he called unto him his disciples, and saith unto them, Verily I say unto you, That this poor widow hath cast more in, than all they which have cast into the treasure; For all they did cast in of their abundance (surplus); but she of her want (out of her poverty) did cast in all that she had, even all her living(whole livelihood)." **Mark 12:43, 44** (KJV)

I considered the widow mite; I saw that what she put in, the others with all their abundance could not measure up to what she gave. She gave in faith. She gave willing. She had no fear. She gave all that she had in spite of her circumstances. She didn't allow her circumstance to cause her to disobey God.   She gave out of love for God. She trusted him for a miracle like He gave the Shunammite Woman in 2 Kings 8:1-6.

As I continued to think on the size of my tithe, the Lord caused a Galloping V number problem to surface that looked like this.

```
5  9  13  17  21          1  4  16  64  256
\ / \ /\ /\ /             \ /\ /\ /\ /
+4  +4  +4  +4            x4  x4  x4  x4
  Increase        vs.      Greatly Increase
```

He then took that and related it to the feeding of the 5000 men, beside women and children.   **(John 6:1-14)**   The power of multiplication was applied to the 5 loaves and 2 fishes to the extent that 12 basketfuls were leftover and from the feeding of the 4000 men, beside women and children 7 basketfuls were leftover **(Matt. 15:32-37)**.

God richly returned to the young boy for not withholding a seed in the time of a great need.   What He did for the hungry crowd and the young boy He desires to do for you – satisfy the need with some left over to share and enjoy!

5

SATAN: THE DEVOURER

"The thief cometh not, except to steal, kill, and destroy:..."
John 10:10a

The Lord has our best interest at heart to multiply us, but Satan's desires and plans are to divide, decrease and bring us to zero. He works to keep us out of our God given inheritance. He is the opposite of everything that is good. Satan is our enemy. And as our enemy he works against us to steal, kill, and destroy. He works to keep us in bondage to sin and bondages in our mind, will, emotion and finances. Satan lives in a spiritual realm and in this spiritual realm are spiritual laws. One of those spiritual laws is: If God's people do not act in accordance with the Word of God; Satan has an open right to enforce his work upon them. His will is to keep us in poverty by keeping the truth hidden from us. The devil knows that the truth is light and if people come into the light of the truth they will be set free from his darkness. Satan wants to keep people in darkness to what

God has for them. If He can keep people in darkness, the people will see God as their enemy. The devil wants people to hate God and blame God for every bad thing that happens in their life. So, whether you're in debt or suffering lack, Satan works to keep you there. He's an instigator. He causes things to happen that prevents you from coming out of debt. He creates problems or mishaps that cause you to borrow or spend money that was needed for some other important obligation. He comes against you and your family's health, car, house, etc., to stir up mishaps and problems that will deplete (exhaust, empty wholly or partly) you. Satan will deplete you of your dreams and the ability to get wealth. He will send laziness and consistent drowsy to bind you. He works to prevent you from moving ahead. And he wants you to blame God for it all!

Satan's plan is to keep us exhausted or empty. He desires to keep us out of our God given inheritance. God does not wish ill will to His people. Whatever our occupation is God wants us to be successful in it. He wants the best for us as any good father does. God desires to restore dreams and visions into us. He wants to restore to us what the enemy stolen. And He wants to do it through our faith and giving.

In **Malachi 3:10, 11** it is written, *"Bring ye all the tithes(a tenth of your income) into the storehouse, that there may be meat in mine house, and prove me now herewith, saith the LORD of host, if I will not open you the windows of heaven, and pour you out a blessing, that there shall not be room enough to receive it. And I will rebuke the devourer (the devil) for your sakes, and he shall not destroy the fruits of your ground; neither shall your vine cast her fruit before the time in the field, saith the LORD of hosts." (KJV)*

It is also written in **II Corinthians 9:6-8** concerning giving of offerings:

"But this I say, He which soweth sparingly shall reap also sparingly; and he which soweth bountifully shall reap also bountifully. Every man according as he purposeth in his heart, so let him give; not grudgingly, or of necessity: for God loveth a cheerful giver. And God is able to make all grace abound toward you; that ye, always having all sufficiency in all things, may abound to every good work:"(KJV)

Our defense against the devourer is to give, and give in a continually rhythm manner, and do it faithfully – even in difficult seasons. If we give a little bit tomorrow and a little bit next month, then we will reap a little bit tomorrow and a little bit next month -- if the devourer doesn't eat it before the next week or month comes in.

When we give in a continually rhythm manner, our fruits will multiply and we will reap in an ongoing manner until the devourer is pushed back. Mishaps and misfortunes will be reduced. The devourer will be pushed back from our family's health – health restored and less sickness. He'll be pushed back from our property -- new and better things with fewer repairs. He'll be pushed back from our finances – higher paying jobs, which reduces lack and borrowing. He'll be pushed back from other areas that surround our life. We'll have more peace of mind. What a blessing!

When we faithfully carry out *v.10*, the Lord will faithfully perform *vv.11&12*. The Lord said He will rebuke the devourer for our sake – and He will. The Lord will snap His whip against Satan. God's whip is a burning flame of fire. The whip to Satan means get back, don't come near, stop right there and this is what you can expect if you try to come near. Can you imagine being snapped with a whip? Imagine what it feels like or does to your flesh. Would you like to have a snap of a whip? No! Neither does Satan. A snap of God's whip turns Satan's work into ashes that the wind carries away. Satan may be mean and cruel, but he's no fool when it comes to the whip of God against him. *"Thou believest that there is one God; thou doest well: the devils also believe, and tremble."* **James 2:19** (KJV)

Only those in the Lord who plant their tithes and offering have a right to bring to God's remembrance of what He said He would do to the devour. Our giving and confessing God's Word to the enemy is an act of faith that God blesses. It produces good results in binding the devourer from our prosperity. It releases increase on our behalf that causes us to enjoy more prosperity in our spirit, mind, emotions, health, finances, businesses, relationships, etc. Prosperity may not happen all at once, but it will happen if we continue on with the Lord. We have to get it started by planting our seeds, watering them with faith (trust) in God, waiting on the blade, the bud, and the fruit and we will reap a harvest; if we faint not. God will rebuke Satan for your sake!

Now, God would not that His children be ignorant. Don't be disillusion that all of your problems are going to vanish overnight, and you'll never have troubles again, for that would be contrary to God's word, for Jesus said, *"In the world ye shall have tribulation: but be of good cheer; I have overcome the world."* **John 16:33** (KJV)

The Lord said to be of good cheer, He have overcome the world. The Lord is saying, "Because he overcame in the world, He will help us to overcome in this world – cheer up! The devourer doesn't have to overcome you, but you can overcome him through faith in Christ. In Christ Jesus you don't have to confess, nor believe that you are hopeless and helpless. *"For whatsoever is born of God overcometh the world: and this is the victory that overcometh the world, even our faith. Who is he that overcometh the world, but he that believeth that Jesus is the Son of God?"* **I John 5:4, 5** (KJV)

In Christ Jesus we can experience a more abundant life – in our family, health, finances, education, business, etc. We can experience a more abundant life with the Lord than without Him.

Also, we can't blame everything on Satan, because a good percent of our troubles are caused by our own actions, such as; the foods we eat, our life- style, the way we handle money, the way we treat and deal with others, etc.

6

FAVORED WITH WISDOM TO PROFIT

"Wisdom is the principal thing; therefore get wisdom; and with all thy getting get understanding." **Proverbs 4:7**

Why is wisdom important? One answer is found in **Proverbs 8:21,** *"That I may cause those that love me to inherit substance (wealth); and I will fill their treasures."* *(KJV)*

God desires us to have wisdom so He can cause us to inherit substance – tangible and intangible.

[inherit – to come into possession of, esp. by legal succession or will. 2. to receive by genetic transmission from an ancestor.]

God desires to favor us with wisdom so we can inherit the promise of our ancestor Abraham. For it is through him that God promised that we should be blessed. *"And I will bless them that bless thee, and curse him that curseth thee: and in thee shall all families of the earth be blessed."* **Genesis 12:3** (KJV)

Through our acceptance of Jesus in our heart and accepting His Lordship over our life, we position ourselves to claim possession of our ancestry's promise.

By faith we come into the possession of wealth through the sacrificial blood of Jesus Christ. We have been redeemed from the legal hold of the law of poverty through the power of Christ's blood.

"Christ hath redeemed us from the curse of the law, being made a curse for us: for it is written, Cursed Is Every One That Hangeth On A Tree:" That the blessing of Abraham might come on the Gentiles through Jesus Christ; that we might receive the promise of the Spirit through faith." **Galatians 3:13, 14** (KJV)

We are presently legal successions of wealth in every aspect of the word – from spiritual to financial and everything we can imagine that is good and pure. Today, we can claim our inheritance! Today God desires to bring us into a wealthy place!

Christians, God wants to give you wisdom and power so you can take hold of your inheritance. If any of you lacks wisdom and the ability to inherit substance, ask God for it in faith.

"If any of you lack wisdom, let him ask of God that giveth to all men liberally and without reproach and it shall be given him. But let him ask in faith, not doubting. For he that doubts is like a wave of the sea driven with the wind and tossed. For let not that man think that he shall receive any thing of the Lord." **James 1:5-7** (KJV)

Your faith can cause God to favor you with wisdom to start a business; record songs; write books; invent things; create things; or become that leader; teacher; architect, or that person you dreamt of becoming as your power to inherit your inheritance. Do not doubt the ability of God to fulfill His promise to you. Doubt will keep the blessing hidden, but faith will reveal it. You will never know the greatness that is in you until you take God as your partner. There are powers in you to prosper that are hidden from your knowledge. Powers only Christ can cause to surface. With the wisdom of God, your life can take on a whole new meaning. Those dreams that you dreamt can become reality. You can aspire to new heights in life. You can accomplish those seemly impossible goals or tasks. Those failures can turn into successes.

It is written in the Bible that your life is hid with Christ. Your life is not hidden with a psychic, fortuneteller, medium, astrology or any other work of Satan. Seeking information from these sources is demonic wisdom. Turn from demonic wisdom for it is evil work. It may appear to be good and pure but if it comes through the wrong source it is polluted, and God's blessing is not in it. The Lord warns about seeking help from these sources in **Deuteronomy 18: 10-13,**

"There shall not be found among you any one that maketh his son or his daughter to pass through the fire (Be burned as an offering to an idol), or that useth divination, or an observer of times, or an enchanter, or a witch, or a charmer, or a consulter with familiar spirits, or a wizard, or a necromancer, For all that do these things are an abomination unto the LORD: and because of these abominations the LORD thy God doth drive them out from before thee. Thou shall be perfect (blameless) with the LORD thy God." (KJV)

It is written in **I Corinthians 2:9** *"Eye hath not seen, nor ear heard, neither have entered into the heart of man, the things which God hath prepared for them that love Him."* If you are in the poor house of life, at this time, and can't see a pathway out; If you have searched the halls of your mind and keep coming up empty; If no worth while ideal have enter your mind that you may obtain financial increase; If your way of increase have failed over and over again; If the power to obtain wealth seems to be shut up in your life, and the

44

secret to wealth is not revealed to you -- don't be dismayed be encouraged, **"Your redemption draws near!"**

God has already prepared an abundance of good things for you. Through Jesus and faith in Him your pathway can be revealed. Not only will the pathway be open for you but God will also cause wisdom to enter into your spirit in such a way that you will be guided by the Spirit on what to do or get involved in. You can know what God already knows. He knows what venture he has for you. He is the All-Wise God!

If the pathway God has prepared for you and planned for you, regarding your financial prosperity, have not entered into your spirit in a guiding way, then ask and seek God's favor. God will give you wisdom that will cause the eye to perceive, the ear to listen and the intelligent to know what to do to inherit your share of the promised wealth.

God will also reveal a pathway by his Spirit through an anointed Prophet/Prophetess, as He did through Elisha in the Miracle of the Increase of the Widow's Olive Oil in **2 Kings 4:1-7**

"One of the wives of a disciple of the prophets called to Elisha, "Sir, my husband is dead! You know how he feared the LORD. Now a creditor has come to take my two children as slaves." Elisha asked her, 'What should I do for you? Tell

me, what do you have in your house?" She answered, "I have nothing in the house except a jar of olive oil." Elisha said, "Borrow many empty containers from all your neighbors. Then close the door behind you and your children, and pour oil into all those containers. When one is full, set it aside." So she left him and closed the door behind her and her children. The children kept bringing containers to her, and she kept pouring. When the containers were full, she told her son, "Bring me another container." He told her, "There are no more containers." So the olive oil stopped flowing. She went and told the man of God. He said, "Sell the oil, and pay your debt. The rest is for you and your children."(GWS)

Don't limit God to just the Prophets and Prophetess, for God reveal things to other anointed men and women by the G*ift of the Spirit* of the *word of knowledge* (supernatural information revealed by God that you otherwise would not have known).

And don't put your dependence upon another anointed person, for you have a personal relationship with the Lord and The Anointed One lives in you. God may very well reveal things to you by the Holy Spirit that lives in you.

"But ye have an unction (anointing) from the Holy One, and ye know all things. But the anointing which ye have received of him abideth in you, and ye need not that any man teach you: but as the same anointing teacheth you of all

things, and is truth, and is no lie, and even as it hath taught you, ye shall abide in him." **I John 2:20,27** (KJV)

The things that our eyes have not seen; the things that our ears have not heard; the things that have not entered into our heart what God has prepared for us; the Spirit will make known...: *"The Spirit searches everything, especially the deep (hidden) things of God."* **I Corinthians 2:10b**

The Spirit delights in revealing the hidden things of God, including His plan for your prosperity. For when He reveals God's things: Jesus is glorified. Jesus' work (crucifixion death) is honored. The Spirit delights in glorifying the Son. If we love God and obey His commands, we can expect to receive that which we have asked of Him. We can expect to receive wisdom (power) to prosper.

It is written in **I Corinthians** chapter two, *"that we have receive the spirit which is of God; that we might* <u>*know*</u> *the things that are freely given to us of God."* *(KJV)*

> *know* – 1. to perceive directly with the senses or mind;
> 3. to have a practical understanding of.

When we received the baptism of the Holy Spirit, we received the Spirit we asked for. We didn't ask for an evil spirit but the Holy Spirit. The Holy Spirit is the spirit God sent to live in us that we might through His Spirit <u>know</u> (have a practical understanding of) how to take hold of wealth – even whole person wealth – and all things that He has freely given us. Through the indwelling Spirit the wisdom and power is in us, but it takes communicating with the Lord, faith, and action to produce it.

It is written in **I John 2:20, 27** *"The Holy One has anointed you, so all of you have knowledge. The anointing you received from Christ lives in you. You don't need anyone to teach you something else. Instead, Christ's anointing teaches you about everything. His anointing is true and contains no lie. So live in Christ as he taught you to do."(GWS)*

Christians, the Anointed One that lives in you will guide you, teach you, and instruct you on your journey to prosperity. He may guide you to return to school. For He says in **Isaiah 48:17,** *"This is what the LORD, your Defender, the Holy One of Israel, says: I am the LORD your God. I teach you what is best for you. I lead you where you should go."(GWS)*

We fail or miss it so many times on gaining prosperity, because we try to follow our own way or another's way rather than God's way. What Sue came and told you worked for Sue but it didn't work for you. Find out what God has for you – Sue did! We rely too heavily on our own knowledge to get us there and refuse to seek or receive what God has. We need to lighten up off our own knowledge and seek God's knowledge; what He has is better. We fool ourselves when we think we are wiser than God. When we trust in our knowledge and ability to deliver us, we sin against God and that is accounted as evil in the Lord's eyes. Leaning on our own wisdom is evil and puts us in league with Satan. When we're in league with Satan we're in league with poverty, shortage, lack, consistent failure, and debt. Our own wisdom can destroy our wholeness. We need to repent and turn from this evil. Now, we can have confidence in ourselves that we can do things, for I believe there is greatness in each one of us, but not acknowledging or rejecting God's hand in it reveals pride in us. Godly wisdom says in **Proverbs 3:5-7** *"Trust the LORD with all your heart, and do not rely on your own understanding. In all your ways acknowledge him, and he will make your path smooth. Do not consider yourself wise, Fear the LORD, and turn away from evil."(GWS)*

Pride is evil and it is of the evil one –Satan. God cannot and will not prosper a prideful person. If that person is prospering it is not of God. God does not prosper prideful people. God's first interest is in the salvation of their souls not in sending them financial prosperity. God keeps his distance from prideful people. He sees them only from a distance and the hole – unseen to them – that they shall fall in.

"Even though the LORD is high above, he sees humble people close up and he recognizes arrogant people from a distance." **Psalm 138:6** (GWS)

"Pride precedes a disaster and an arrogant attitude precedes a fall." **Proverbs 16:18** (GWS)

"A person's pride will humiliate him, but a humble spirit gains honor." **Proverbs 29:23** *(GWS)*

God can and will favor the humble person and honor him with his share of the promised inheritance. The prideful may be spreading themselves like a green bay tree, but sooner or later they will be cut down. Their leaves will wither and their trunk and roots will die.

I believe the wisdom that we need to prosper wholly is already deposited in us. I believe that spending time with God in prayer, praise, worship and giving of tithes and offerings will bring it to light. Be opened to the Holy Spirit leading; He may lead you to fast. But even if he doesn't and you fast anyway God will reward you openly. Your open reward could very well be the wisdom you need to move from here to there to obtain you bless inheritance. It could be the key that unlocks the door of Godly favor.

When Jesus – through the Holy Spirit – reveals your pathway to financial heritance, there should be Godly peace in your spirit that flows to your mind. If you don't have an assurance of peace about it, continue regularly in prayer until that peace comes. Don't proceed without it. *"Never worry about anything. But in every situation let God know what you need in prayers and requests while giving thanks. Then God's peace, which goes beyond anything we can imagine, will guard your thoughts and emotions through Christ Jesus."* **Philippians 4:6** (GWS)

Christians, don't limit your life to just financial increase, for God wants you to be made whole. Seek whole person prosperity in every area of your life. Your being is not just flesh but spirit also. You have a mind, emotions, and a will that need to be made whole. God has made provision for your whole person. So seek wholeness!

CONCLUSION

AWAKE, OH MY SOUL!

Awake, oh my soul and arise to the call! Sleep no longer, but arise! Possess your inheritance! Reach out, oh my soul, and by wisdom take hold of what is rightly yours! Oh my soul, sit not as a beggar! Oh my soul, be strengthen with might! Rise up and overcome! Take spear and sword and strike! Wake up, rise up and run through a troop! Be empowered my soul, and leap over this wall! My soul, be gird with God's strength, for he makes your way to be complete! My soul, your feet are like the feet of a deer! You tread over the roughest of the enemy territory without fear; with each step your feet is made sure! My soul, by the power of God rise up and pursue your enemies until they be overtaken! My soul, rest not in the bonds of slumber! Do not find rest until all thy enemies have been consumed!

Let it be Lord Jesus, let it be!

ABOUT THE AUTHOR

Barbara A. Perry is a teacher of the Word of God. She is senior pastor of Spirit of Prevailing Faith in Aiken, South Carolina. She has been pastoring for over 20 years. She is a Christian author and sole proprietor of Garden 33 Publisher. She is married to Jimmie Perry. She has two daughters: Alice and Samantha and three grandchildren: Da'Shawn, Samara, and Natalie.

Other books by Barbara A. Perry:

Release The Greatness That's Within You

PIAS: Supernatural Sessions

Website: www.garden33publisher.com

Email: pastorbawp@yahoo.com